SLICKETY QUICK

SLICKETY QUICK

POEMS ABOUT SHARKS

Skila Brown

illustrated by
Bob Kolar

CANDLEWICK PRESS

Okay.
We get
it. You're big
and bad and mean.
And you think that
everywhere you go, there
should be scary music.
But really, you're no bully,
just a big attention hog. So
move over. Let another shark
swim to the beat.

Even though there are more than 400 different species of sharks, it is the world's largest predatory fish — the great white shark — that seems to get all the attention. Maybe that's because unlike most sharks, it can lift its head out of the water.

WOBBEGONG

Wibbly wobbly wobbegong,
shagginess drips as he swims along.
On the floor of a cave,
he gives a small wave,
singing his own little carpet song.

Wibbly wobbly wobbegong,
still as an ancient rock all day long.
He'll only bite
when the time is just right—
(yet every fish thinks it's *very* wrong!).

Wobbegongs are also called carpet sharks because they sluggishly wait around on the bottom of the ocean floor. They're so still that sometimes a fish will come up and nibble on one before the wobbegong turns it into dinner!

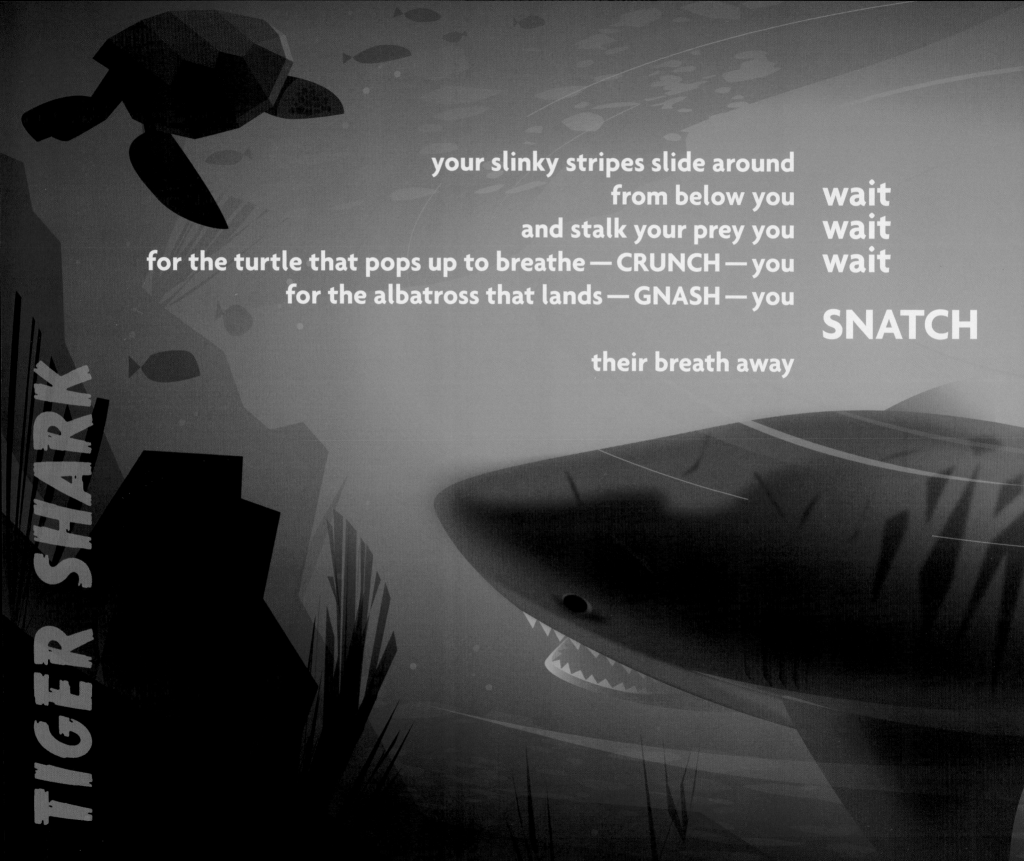

TIGER SHARK

your slinky stripes slide around
from below you   **wait**
and stalk your prey you   **wait**
for the turtle that pops up to breathe — CRUNCH — you   **wait**
for the albatross that lands — GNASH — you

SNATCH

their breath away

Named for the dark stripes on its gray back, the tiger shark enters lagoons and shallow reefs at dusk and uses its strong jaws and teeth to snatch up a meal.

BLUE SHARK

Blue shark, blue shark,
you dip and dive all day.

Pointy snout, bullet nose,
bold eyes that never close,
graceful as the water flows,
bay to bay to bay.

Blue shark, blue shark,
you dip and dive all day.

You dart like an arrow shot—
dot. to dot. to dot. to dot.
Munching on from spot to spot,
prey to prey to prey.

The blue shark is easy to spot, with its bright-blue sides. A female can have large litters of pups — more than 25 at a time!

FRILLED SHARK

Frilled sharks are called living fossils because they have changed so little over millions of years. They feed in caves and crevices deep in the ocean, so we don't see them very often.

Slowly
through the
deepest
blue,
rocking
side to
side,

frilled sharks
swim where
light is
dim and
they can
almost
hide.

Lean and
long, teeth
needle-
strong,
with foggy,
empty
eyes.

Swollen
gills, all
hooks and
frills, a
snakelike
fossil
prize.

COOKIE-CUTTER SHARK

Swimming, slick, swimming, stick. Stuck on the butt of supper. Twist twist twist twist twist. It's all over now — slickety quick. Just a bit of lunch. Circle of crunch. Cut cut cut. Stuck on the butt of supper.

Cookie-cutter sharks are small: males are about 16 ½ inches/ 42 centimeters long, and females are about 22 inches/56 centimeters long. They get their name from the marks they leave behind. They bite their prey (usually a large fish, whale, or dolphin), then spin around, removing a hunk of flesh and leaving a cookie-shaped hole in their victim.

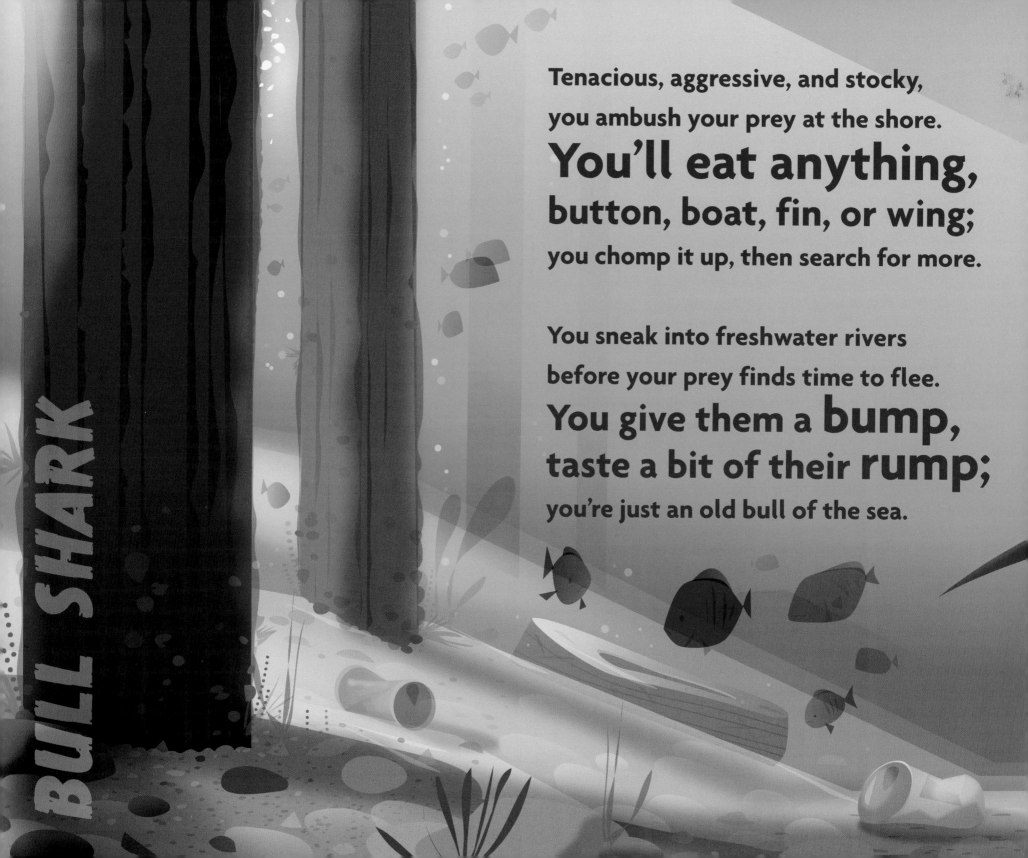

BULL SHARK

Tenacious, aggressive, and stocky,
you ambush your prey at the shore.
You'll eat anything,
button, boat, fin, or wing;
you chomp it up, then search for more.

You sneak into freshwater rivers
before your prey finds time to flee.
You give them a bump,
taste a bit of their rump;
you're just an old bull of the sea.

Bull sharks are unpredictable animals. They head-butt their prey before taking a bite of them and can even tolerate freshwater, sometimes swimming into rivers!

The nurse shark has a curled, hinged mouth that makes a sucking noise, much like the sound of a nursing baby, when the shark hunts for prey on the sandy bottom of the ocean floor.

NURSE SHARK

R200353|403

Two long whiskers — like a frown. Little mustache drips right down.

Vacuums creatures all around, cleaning up the whole sea town.

MAKO SHARK

Mako sharks hunt their prey by swimming below them and lunging up as fast as 20 miles/32 kilometers per hour, taking their meals by surprise.

**Underwater cheetah,
muscle torpedo,
silver bullet of the sea —
that tuna never *hadachance*.**

Deep down in the ocean, in the belly of the dark,

are the rubbery lips of the megamouth shark,

swishing on the plankton that he swallows all day

from his home at the bottom, where he swims in the gray.

His monster of a mouth opens wide in a roar

that's a lonely whisper from the ocean floor.

At the bottom of the sea, in the belly of the dark,

in the cold and the quiet, lives the megamouth shark.

Discovered in 1976, megamouth sharks are so rare that only a few have ever been seen. This is because they spend their days in deep water, swimming to shallow water only at night, when krill move to the surface.

GOBLIN SHARK

When you see a goblin glow, you'll think:
Nice pink!

When it swims from side to side to pose:
Long nose!

When it flips and dives and points to south:
No mouth?

But when the jaws from down below unhinge:

You'll cringe.

One of the rarest species, the goblin shark is unusual, with its bubble-gum pink color and its long flat snout that hides its mouth. Its jaws are so flexible that when it moves to take a bite, its mouth pops out!

WHALE SHARK

In water she dangles, and bubbles and jangles, and

blinks her mouth right up at me. Her back spots they shimmer, her tail getting dimmer, the silkiest wave of the sea.

The largest species of fish, whale sharks are slow-moving, speckled filter feeders that swim in open waters. They are docile creatures and will often let humans swim around them.

ANGEL SHARK

Flat body, little crêpe.
Who would be afraid
of angel wings?

Wiggle down to the ground,
under sand, and wait —
see what the water brings.

Look what's there, unaware:
a fish — unsafe!
Poor delicious things.

Flat body, little crêpe.
Devil tail that shakes
those angel wings.

The angel shark is no angel! It can bury its flat "wings" in sand or mud and hide on the ocean floor. Then it waits for a fish to swim by so it can burst up and catch it in its traplike jaws.

HAMMERHEAD SHARK
(A POEM FOR TWO VOICES)

He enters the reef, the ballroom, and swims,	She waits at the reef, the ballroom,
	with her friends,
searching for a partner.	searching for a partner.
He knows the right moves to show that he wants to dance: tilt to the side,	She knows the right moves to show that she wants to dance:
	swim up and down,
white belly flash,	blinking her softness,
swimming at an angle	an angel.
The first one comes near, and tickles his chin, but something feels off.	The first one comes near, she nibbles his skin, but something feels off.
He shakes his head.	
	She swims away.
But then he sees another. He tilts.	But then she sees another.
	She nods.
Now it's just the two of them, swimming away into the night,	Now it's just the two of them, swimming away,
	love at first
bite.	bite.

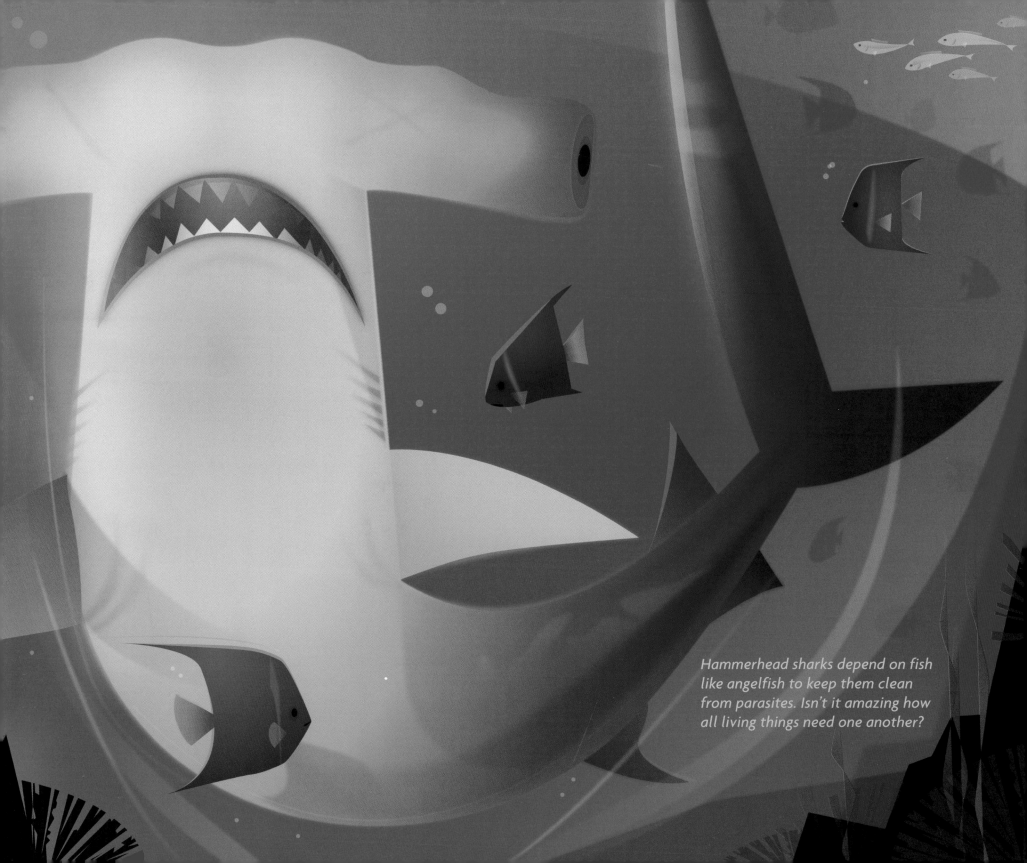

Hammerhead sharks depend on fish like angelfish to keep them clean from parasites. Isn't it amazing how all living things need one another?

For Isaac, who taught me all about sharks
S. B.

For Nicholas, who survived the shark bite
B. K.

First edition 2016

Library of Congress Catalog Card Number 2014960103
ISBN 978-0-7636-6543-2

15 16 17 18 19 20 APS 10 9 8 7 6 5 4 3 2 1

Printed in Humen, Dongguan, China

This book was typeset in Agenda.
The illustrations were created digitally.

Candlewick Press
99 Dover Street
Somerville, Massachusetts 02144

visit us at www.candlewick.com